COLDEST CLIMATES

BY MARISSA KIRKMAN

Apex is distributed by North Star Editions:
sales@northstareditions.com | 888-417-0195

Produced for Apex by Red Line Editorial.

Photographs ©: Shutterstock Images, cover, 1, 4–5, 6–7, 8–9, 10–11, 12, 13, 14–15, 18–19, 24–25, 26, 27, 29; iStockphoto, 16–17, 18, 22–23; Louise Murray/Science Source, 20–21

Library of Congress Control Number: 2022919859

ISBN
978-1-63738-528-9 (hardcover)
978-1-63738-582-1 (paperback)
978-1-63738-689-7 (ebook pdf)
978-1-63738-636-1 (hosted ebook)

Printed in the United States of America
Mankato, MN
082023

NOTE TO PARENTS AND EDUCATORS

Apex books are designed to build literacy skills in striving readers. Exciting, high-interest content attracts and holds readers' attention. The text is carefully leveled to allow students to achieve success quickly. Additional features, such as bolded glossary words for difficult terms, help build comprehension.

TABLE OF CONTENTS

CHAPTER 1

COLDEST PLACE ON EARTH

A cold wind blows over Antarctica. The temperature drops below −40 degrees Fahrenheit (−40°C). Snow swirls in the air.

Antarctica is a continent near Earth's South Pole. It is covered in ice and snow.

Emperor penguins huddle together. Their bodies have layers of fat and feathers that trap heat to keep them warm.

Emperor penguins live in groups called colonies. Some groups include thousands of penguins.

PENGUIN DADS

Emperor penguins lay eggs just before winter. Males care for the eggs for around two months. Each male holds an egg on his feet. A flap of skin covers the egg. It keeps the egg warm.

Swimming helps Weddell seals stay warm. Wind can make air above the water very cold.

A Weddell seal dives under the ice. It looks for food. A minke whale swims nearby. Both animals have thick **blubber**. It keeps them warm in the freezing water.

FAST FACT

Weddell seals live farther south than any other kind of seal.

CHAPTER 2

STAYING WARM ON LAND

Antarctica and the **Arctic** are both very cold. Animals in these places often have thick fur. Polar bears are one example. Their huge paws help them walk on ice.

In the summer, an Arctic fox's white fur will turn brown. This helps it blend in with plants.

The Arctic fox uses its bushy tail like a blanket. Arctic hares dig **burrows** in the snow. Both animals have white fur. This color helps them blend in.

BODY SHAPE

Many Arctic animals have stocky bodies with short **limbs**. This body shape helps them stay warm. When fewer body parts stick out in the icy wind, less heat escapes.

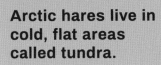

Arctic hares live in cold, flat areas called tundra.

Musk oxen have two layers of fur. The thick bottom layer traps heat. The long top layer blocks snow.

FAST FACT

Arctic winters are around −35 degrees Fahrenheit (−37°C).

Musk oxen often sit or stand with their backs to the wind.

CHAPTER 3

STAYING WARM IN WATER

Narwhals live in the Arctic Ocean. The cold water is often covered with ice. Blubber keeps narwhals warm.

A narwhal has a long tooth called a tusk that sticks

Bowhead whales can stay underwater for more than 30 minutes. Then they come up to breathe.

Bowhead whales also live in the Arctic. Their blubber can be 2 feet (61 cm) thick. They use their big heads to break ice. They make holes to breathe air.

TRAPPING HEAT

Walruses swim in very cold water. Their blubber traps heat. And their blood vessels **constrict**. This makes their skin look pale. It also helps their bodies stay warmer.

Up to one-third of a walrus's weight comes from its blubber.

Greenland sharks can dive up to 7,200 feet (2,200 m) underwater.

Greenland sharks live in cold, deep waters. Their bodies contain chemicals that keep their blood from freezing. **Proteins** in the blood of Arctic cod and Antarctic ice fish also prevent freezing.

FAST FACT

The chemicals in a Greenland shark's body make it poisonous.

CHAPTER 4

BIRDS IN COLD CLIMATES

Arctic terns are found in both Antarctica and the Arctic. They **migrate** between both places. The birds fly back and forth every year.

Arctic terns travel about 25,000 miles (40,000 km)

Adélie penguins live in Antarctica. They huddle together to keep warm. They hunt in groups, too. This helps them stay safe from **predators**.

Adélie penguins live
on or near sea ice.

Snow petrels are sea birds. They catch fish near cracks in the Antarctic ice.

Snow petrels live near the South Pole. They build nests in cliffs. The rock protects them from cold winds.

FLUFFY FEATHERS

Some snowy owls live near the North Pole. Thick feathers keep the birds warm. The feathers are also heavy. Snowy owls are among the heaviest owls. They often weigh 4 pounds (1.8 kg).

A snowy owl even has feathers on its feet.

COMPREHENSION QUESTIONS

Write your answers on a separate piece of paper.

1. Write a sentence that explains how land animals stay warm in cold climates.

2. Would you rather visit the North Pole or the South Pole? Why?

3. Which bird migrates between the Arctic and Antarctica?

    A. snow petrel

    B. emperor penguin

    C. Arctic tern

4. How does having white fur help an animal survive in a snowy climate?

    A. White fur helps the animal hide from predators.

    B. White fur stays clean in the snow.

    C. White fur soaks up heat from the sun.

5. What does **bushy** mean in this book?

*The Arctic fox uses its **bushy** tail like a blanket.*

    A. thick and fluffy

    B. covered with small plants

    C. thin and prickly

6. What does **huddle** mean in this book?

*They **huddle** together to keep warm. They hunt in groups, too.*

    A. make a plan

    B. jump up and down

    C. gather close together

Answer key on page 32.

GLOSSARY

Arctic
The very cold area near the North Pole.

blubber
A thick layer of fat.

burrows
Tunnels or holes that animals use as homes.

constrict
To get smaller and tighter.

hemisphere
One half of the world. Earth's top half is the northern hemisphere. The southern hemisphere is the bottom half.

limbs
Parts of the body used for moving or grasping, such as arms, legs, wings, or flippers.

migrate
To move from one part of the world to another.

predators
Animals that hunt and eat other animals.

proteins
Substances that the body needs to live and grow.

TO LEARN MORE

BOOKS

Earley, Christina. *Adaptations.* Coral Springs, FL: Seahorse Publishing, 2023.

Ridley, Sarah. *Who Ate the Penguin?: An Ocean Food Chain.* New York: Crabtree Publishing, 2020.

Rustad, Martha E. H. *Animals of the Arctic Tundra.* North Mankato, MN: Capstone Press, 2022.

ONLINE RESOURCES

Visit **www.apexeditions.com** to find links and resources related to this title.

ABOUT THE AUTHOR

Marissa Kirkman is a writer and editor who lives in Illinois. She enjoys reading about animals, science, and history.

INDEX

ANSWER KEY:
1. Answers will vary; 2. Answers will vary; 3. C; 4. A; 5. A; 6. C